AUDIO ACCESS INCLUDED

QUEEN
UPDATED EDITION

T0071386

PLAYBACK+
Speed • Pitch • Balance • Loop

To access audio, visit:
www.halleonard.com/mylibrary

Enter Code
7249-5043-0201-7715

© Jorgen Angel/CTSIMAGES

Audio arrangements by Peter Deneff

ISBN 978-1-5400-3847-0

HAL•LEONARD®

Visit Hal Leonard Online at
www.halleonard.com

Contact us:
Hal Leonard
7777 West Bluemound Road
Milwaukee, WI 53213
Email: info@halleonard.com

In Europe, contact:
Hal Leonard Europe Limited
42 Wigmore Street
Marylebone, London, W1U 2RN
Email: info@halleonardeurope.com

In Australia, contact:
Hal Leonard Australia Pty. Ltd.
4 Lentara Court
Cheltenham, Victoria, 3192 Australia
Email: info@halleonard.com.au

ANOTHER ONE BITES THE DUST

CELLO

Words and Music by
JOHN DEACON

CRAZY LITTLE THING CALLED LOVE

CELLO

Words and Music by
FREDDIE MERCURY

BICYCLE RACE

CELLO

Words and Music by
FREDDIE MERCURY

BOHEMIAN RHAPSODY

CELLO

Words and Music by
FREDDIE MERCURY

FAT BOTTOMED GIRLS

CELLO

Words and Music by
BRIAN MAY

I WANT IT ALL

CELLO

Words and Music by FREDDIE MERCURY,
BRIAN MAY, ROGER TAYLOR
and JOHN DEACON

DON'T STOP ME NOW

CELLO

Words and Music by
FREDDIE MERCURY

I WANT TO BREAK FREE

CELLO

Words and Music by
JOHN DEACON

PLAY THE GAME

CELLO

Words and Music by
FREDDIE MERCURY

KILLER QUEEN

CELLO

Words and Music by
FREDDIE MERCURY

RADIO GA GA

CELLO

Words and Music by
ROGER TAYLOR

SAVE ME

CELLO

Words and Music by
BRIAN MAY

SOMEBODY TO LOVE

CELLO

Words and Music by
FREDDIE MERCURY

UNDER PRESSURE

CELLO

Words and Music by FREDDIE MERCURY,
JOHN DEACON, BRIAN MAY,
ROGER TAYLOR and DAVID BOWIE

WE ARE THE CHAMPIONS

Words and Music by
FREDDIE MERCURY

CELLO

WE WILL ROCK YOU

CELLO

Words and Music by
BRIAN MAY

YOU'RE MY BEST FRIEND

CELLO

Words and Music by
JOHN DEACON